FINDING RELEVANCE IN THE OLD TESTAMENT

A four-week course to help people read and
understand the Old Testament for themselves.

by
Susan L. Lingo and Bob Buller

Apply·It·To·Life™

Adult

BIBLE CURRICULUM
from **Group**

Group
Loveland, Colorado

Apply·It·To·Life™

Adult

BIBLE CURRICULUM

Group

Finding Relevance in the Old Testament
Copyright © 1996 Group Publishing, Inc.

Credits
Chief Creative Officer: Joani Schultz
Senior Editor: Paul Woods
Copy Editor: Janis Sampson
Art Director: Lisa Chandler
Computer Graphic Artist: Ray Tollison
Illustrator: Rex Bohn
Cover Designer: Liz Howe
Cover Photographer: Craig DeMartino

ISBN 1-55945-523-3
10 9 8 7 6 5 4 3 2 1   05 04 03 02 01 00 99 98 97 96
Printed in the United States of America.

C O N T E N T S

Introduction

Apply-It-To-Life™ Adult Bible Curriculum is a series of four-week study courses designed to help you facilitate powerful lessons that will help class members grow in faith. Use this course with
- Sunday school classes,
- home study groups,
- weekday Bible study groups,
- men's Bible studies,
- women's Bible studies, and
- family classes.

The variety of courses gives the adult student a broad coverage of topical, life-related issues and significant biblical topics. In addition, as the name of the series implies, every lesson helps the adult student apply Scripture to his or her life.

Each course in Apply-It-To-Life Adult Bible Curriculum provides four lessons on different aspects of one topic. In each course, you also receive Fellowship and Outreach Specials connected to the month's topic. They provide outreach activities, suggestions for building closer relationships in your class, and even a party idea!

WHAT MAKES APPLY-IT-TO-LIFE™ ADULT BIBLE CURRICULUM UNIQUE?

Teaching as Jesus Taught

Jesus was a master teacher. With Apply-It-To-Life Adult Bible Curriculum, you'll use the same teaching methods and principles that Jesus used:
- **Active Learning.** Think back on an important lesson you've learned in life. Did you learn it from reading about it? from hearing about it? from something you did? Chances are, the most important lessons you've learned came from things you experienced. That's what active learning is—learning by doing. Active learning leads students through activities and experiences that help them understand important principles, messages, and ideas. It's a discovery process that helps people internalize and remember what they learn.

Jesus often used active learning. One of the most vivid examples is his washing of his disciples' feet. In Apply-It-To-Life Adult Bible Curriculum, the teacher might remove his or her shoes and socks, then read aloud the foot-washing passage from John 13, or the teacher might choose to actually wash people's feet. Participants won't soon forget it. Active learning uses simple activities to teach profound lessons.

● **Interactive Learning.** Interactive learning means learning through small-group interaction and discussion. Each person is actively involved in discovering God's truth. Interactive learning puts people in pairs, trios, or foursomes to involve everyone in the learning experience. It takes active learning a step further by having people who have gone through an experience teach others what they've learned.

Jesus often helped cement the learning from an experience by questioning people—sometimes in small groups—about what had happened. He regularly questioned his followers and his opponents, forcing them to think and to discuss among themselves what he was teaching them. After washing his disciples' feet, the first thing Jesus did was ask the disciples if they understood what he had done. After the foot-washing activity, the teacher might form small groups and have people discuss how they felt when the leader removed his or her shoes and socks. Then group members might compare those feelings and the learning involved to what the disciples must have experienced.

● **Biblical Depth.** Apply-It-To-Life Adult Bible Curriculum recognizes that most people are ready to go below the surface to better understand the deeper truths of the Bible. Therefore, the activities and studies go beyond an "easy answer" approach to Christian education and lead adults to grapple with difficult issues from a biblical perspective.

In the Bible Basis, you'll find information that will help you understand the Scriptures you're dealing with. Within the class-time section of the lesson, thought-provoking activities and discussions lead adults to new depths of biblical understanding. "Bible Insights" within the lesson give pertinent information that will bring the Bible to life for you and your class members. In-class handouts give adults significant Bible information and challenge them to search for and discover biblical truths for themselves. Finally, the "For Even Deeper Discussion" sections provide questions that will lead your class members to new and deeper levels of insight and application.

No one questions the depth of Jesus' teachings or the effectiveness of his teaching methods. This curriculum follows Jesus' example and helps people probe the depths of the Bible in a way no other adult curriculum does.

● **Bible Application.** Jesus didn't stop with helping people understand truth. It wasn't enough that the rich young ruler knew all the right answers. Jesus wanted him to take action on what he knew. In the same way, Apply-It-To-Life Adult Bible Curriculum encourages a response in people's lives. That's why this curriculum is called "Apply-It-To-Life"! Depth of understanding means little if the truths of Scripture don't zing into people's hearts. Each lesson brings home one point and encourages people to consider the changes they might make in response.

● **One Purpose.** In each study, every activity works toward communicating and applying the same point. People may discover other new truths, but the study doesn't load them down with a mass of information. Sometimes less is more. When lessons try to teach too much, they often fail to teach anything. Even Jesus limited his teaching to what he felt people could really learn and apply (John 16:12). Apply-It-To-Life Adult Bible Curriculum makes sure that class members thoroughly understand and apply one point each week.

● **Variety.** Jesus constantly varied his teaching methods. One day he would have a serious discussion with his disciples about who he was, and another day he'd baffle them by turning water into wine. What he didn't do was allow them to become bored with what he had to teach them.

Any kind of study can become less than exciting if the leader and students do everything the same way week after week. Apply-It-To-Life Adult Bible Curriculum varies activities and approaches to keep everyone's interest level high each week. In one class, you might have people in small groups "put themselves in the disciples' sandals" and experience something of the confusion of Jesus' death and resurrection. In another lesson, class members may experience problems in communication and examine how such problems can damage relationships.

● **Relevance.** People today want to know how to live successfully right now. They struggle with living as authentic Christians at work, in the family, and in the community. They want to know how the Bible can help them live faithful lives—how it can help them face the difficulties of living in today's culture. Apply-It-To-Life Adult Bible Curriculum bridges the gap between biblical truth and the "real world" issues of people's lives. Jesus didn't discuss with his followers the eschatological significance of Ezekiel's wheels, and Apply-It-To-Life Adult Bible Curriculum won't either! Courses and studies in this curriculum focus on the real needs of people and help them discover answers in Scripture that will help meet those needs.

● **A Nonthreatening Atmosphere.** In many adult classes, people feel intimidated because they're new Christians or because they don't have the Bible knowledge they think they should have. Jesus sometimes intimidated those who opposed him, but he consistently treated his followers with understanding and respect. We want people in church to experience the same understanding and respect Jesus' followers experienced. With Apply-It-To-Life Adult Bible Curriculum, no one is embarrassed for not knowing or understanding as much as someone else. In fact, the interactive learning process minimizes the differences between those with vast Bible knowledge and those with little Bible knowledge. Lessons often begin with nonthreatening, sharing questions and move slowly toward more depth. Whatever their level of knowledge or commitment, class members will work together to discover biblical truths that can affect their lives.

● **A Group That Cares.** Jesus chose 12 people who learned from him together. That group practically lived together—sharing one another's hurts, joys, and ambitions. Sometimes Jesus divided the 12 into smaller groups and worked with just three or four at a time.

Adults today long for a close-knit group with whom they can share personal needs and joys. Activities in this curriculum will help class members get to know one another better and care for one another more as they study the Bible and apply its truths to their lives. As people reveal their thoughts and feelings to one another, they'll grow closer and develop more commitment to the group. And they'll be encouraging one another along the way!

● **An Element of Delight.** We don't often think about Jesus' ministry in this way, but he often brought fun and delight to his followers. Remember the time he raised Peter's mother-in-law or the time he sat happily with children on his lap? How about the joy and excitement at his triumphal entry into Jerusalem or the time he helped his disciples catch a boatload of fish—after they'd fished all night with no success?

People learn more when they're having fun. So within Apply-It-To-Life Adult Bible Curriculum, elements of fun and delight pop up often. And sometimes adding fun is as simple as using a carrot for a pretend microphone!

Taking the Fear out of Teaching

Teachers love Apply-It-To-Life Adult Bible Curriculum because it makes teaching much less stressful. Lessons in this curriculum...

● **are easy to teach.** Interactive learning frees the teacher from being a dispenser of information to serve as a facilitator of learning. Teachers can spend class time guiding people to discover and apply biblical truths. The studies provide clear, understandable Bible background; easy-to-prepare learning experiences; and thought-provoking discussion questions.

● **can be prepared quickly.** Lessons in Apply-It-To-Life Adult Bible Curriculum are logical and clear. There's no sorting through tons of information to figure out the lesson. In 30 minutes, a busy teacher can easily read a lesson and prepare to teach it. In addition, optional and For Extra Time activities allow the teacher to tailor the lesson to the class. And the thorough instructions and questions will guide even an inexperienced teacher through each powerful lesson.

● **let everyone share in the class' success.** With Apply-It-To-Life Adult Bible Curriculum, the teacher is one of the participants. The teacher still guides the class, but the burden is not as heavy. Everyone participates and adds to the study's effectiveness. So when the study has an impact, everyone shares in that success.

● **lead the teacher to new discoveries.** Each lesson is designed to help the teacher first discover a biblical truth. And most teachers will make additional discoveries as they prepare each lesson. In class, the teacher will discover even more as other adults share what they have found. As with any type of teaching, the teacher will likely learn more than anyone else in the class!

● **provide relevant information to class members.** Photocopiable handouts are designed to help people better understand or interpret Bible passages. And the handouts make teaching easier because the teacher can often refer to them for small-group discussion questions and instructions.

First familiarize yourself with an Apply-It-To-Life Adult Bible Curriculum lesson. The following explanations will help you understand how the lesson elements work together.

Lesson Elements

● The **Opening** maps out the lesson's agenda and introduces the topic. Sometimes this activity will help people get better acquainted as they begin to explore the topic together.

● The **Bible Exploration and Application** activities will help people discover what the Bible says about the topic and how the lesson's point applies to their lives. In these varied activities, class members find answers to the "So what?" question. They discover the relevance of the Scriptures and commit to growing closer to God.

You may use one or both of the options in this section. They are designed to stand alone or to work together. Both present the same point in different ways. "For Even Deeper Discussion" questions appear at the end of each activity in this section. Use these questions whenever you feel they might be particularly helpful for your class.

● The **Closing** pulls everything in the lesson together and often funnels the lesson's message into a time of reflection and prayer.

● The **For Extra Time** section is just that. Use it when you've completed the lesson and still have time left or when you've used one Bible Exploration and Application option and don't have time to do the other. Or you might plan to use it instead of another option.

When you put all the sections together, you get a lesson that's fun and easy to teach. Plus, participants will learn truths they'll remember and apply to their daily lives.

Guidelines for a Successful Adult Class

● **Be a facilitator, not a lecturer.** Your job is to direct the activities and facilitate the discussions. You become a choreographer of sorts: someone who gets everyone else involved in the discussion and keeps the discussion on track.

● **Teach adults how to form small groups.** Help adults form groups of four, three, or two—whatever the activity calls for. Small-group sharing allows for more discussion and involvement by all participants. It's not as threatening or scary to open up to two people as it would be to 20 or 200!

Some leaders decide not to form small groups because they want to hear everybody's ideas. The intention is good, but some people just won't talk in a large group. Use a "report back" time after small-group discussions to gather the best responses from all groups.

Try creative group-forming methods to help everyone in the class get to know one another. For example, have class members form groups with others who are wearing the same color, shop at the same grocery store, were born the same month, or like the same season of the year.

● **Encourage relationship building.** George Barna, in his insightful book about the church, *The Frog in the Kettle,* explains that adults today have a strong need to develop friendships. In a society of high-tech toys, "personal" computers, and lonely commutes, people long for positive human contact. That's where our church classes and groups can jump in. Help adults form friendships through your class. What's discovered in a classroom setting will be better applied when friends support each other outside the classroom. In fact, the relationships begun in your class may be as important as the truths you help your adults learn.

● **Expect the unexpected.** Active learning is an adventure that doesn't always take you where you think you're going. Be open to the different directions the Holy Spirit may lead your class. When something goes wrong or an unexpected emotion is aroused, take advantage of this teachable moment. Ask probing questions; follow up on someone's deep need.

What should you do if people go off on a tangent? Don't panic. People learn best when they're engaged in meaningful discussion. And if you get through even one activity, your class will discover the point for the whole lesson. So relax. It's OK if you don't get everything done.

● **Participate—and encourage participation.** Apply-It-To-Life Adult Bible Curriculum is only as interactive as you and your class make it. Jump into discussions yourself, but don't "take over." Encourage everyone to participate. Use "active listening" responses such as rephrasing and summing up what's been said. To get more out of your discussions, use follow-up inquiries such as "Can you tell me more?" "What do you mean by that?" or "What makes you feel that way?" The more people participate, the more they'll discover God's truths for themselves.

● **Trust the Holy Spirit.** All the previous guidelines and the instructions in the lessons will be irrelevant if you ignore the presence of God in your classroom. God sent the Holy Spirit as our helper. As you use this curriculum, ask the Holy Spirit to help you facilitate the lessons. And ask the Holy Spirit to direct your class toward God's truth. Trust that God's Spirit can work through each person's discoveries, not just the teacher's.

How to Use This Course

Before the Four-Week Session

● Read the Course Introduction and This Course at a Glance (pp. 11-12).

● Decide how you'll use the art on the Publicity Page (p. 13) to publicize the course. Prepare fliers, newsletter articles, and posters as needed.

● Look at the Fellowship and Outreach Specials (pp. 63-64) and decide which ones you'll use.

Before Each Lesson

● Read the one-sentence Point, the Objectives, and the Bible Basis for the lesson. The Bible Basis provides background information on the lesson's passages and shows how those passages relate to people today.

● Choose which activities you'll use from the lesson. Remember—it's not necessary to do every activity. Pick the ones that best fit your group and your time allotment.

● Gather necessary supplies and make photocopies of any handouts you intend to use. They're listed in This Lesson at a Glance.

● Read each section of the lesson. Adjust activities as necessary to fit your class size and meeting room, but be careful not to delete all the activity. People learn best when they're actively involved.

● Make one photocopy of the "Apply-It-To-Life This Week!" handout for each class member.

COURSE INTRODUCTION: FINDING RELEVANCE IN THE OLD TESTAMENT

"More people praise the Bible than read it. More read it than understand it, and more understand it than conscientiously follow it."
—Samuel Sandmel

If your class is like most, Sandmel's observation is probably as true of the people you'll be teaching as it is for society as a whole. Thus, although 92 percent of your class members own at least one Bible, only 37 percent of them read it during the past week (George Barna, *Virtual America,* p. 49). Moreover, given the current plague of doctrinal and ethical confusion within our churches and our communities, it seems that many of the people who do read the Bible don't understand it well enough to apply it to their daily lives.

That's where this course can help. Many people shy away from the Bible because they are intimidated by its strange customs and foreign names. And, in all honesty, the Old Testament is usually the most intimidating part of all. But people can read the Old Testament comfortably and confidently when someone shows them how to sift through the confusing details and spot the nuggets of God's truth. Moreover, people can understand and apply the truths of the Old Testament to their lives when they've been taught how to translate the ideas of the biblical text into practical ideals they can use every day. With the guidance provided by this course, people will learn how to read, understand, and follow the truths God has revealed within the Old Testament.

To help your class members read the Old Testament with understanding, this four-week course will introduce them to the central ideas and the most common types of literature found in the Old Testament. Class members will read Old Testament stories to observe how God is active in the world. They'll also examine specific psalms to discover how to pray honestly and investigate portions of the wisdom literature to learn how to think critically. Finally, class members will study the lives and the words of the prophets to find out what a commitment to God really entails. All along the way, people will take the truths that they uncover and apply them to their lives in concrete and meaningful ways. So, by the time they complete this course, your class members will not only praise but also read, understand, and follow Old Testament truth.

This Course at a Glance

Before you dive into the lessons, familiarize yourself with each lesson's point. Then read the Scripture passages.
- Study them to gain insight into the lessons.
- Use them as a basis for your personal devotions.
- Think about how they relate to people's situations today.

Lesson 1: Compelling Stories
The Point: God is active in our world in various ways.
Bible Basis: 1 Samuel 26:1-25 and 2 Chronicles 20:1-30

Lesson 2: Honest Prayers
The Point: God always wants us to tell him exactly how we feel.
Bible Basis: Psalms 13:1-6; 16:1-11; 63:1-11; and 103:1-22

Lesson 3: True Wisdom
The Point: God gave us our minds, and he expects us to use them.
Bible Basis: Proverbs 1:1-7; 24:30-34; and Ecclesiastes 5:18-20; 12:13-14

Lesson 4: Prophetic Insights
The Point: Following God sometimes means challenging the status quo.
Bible Basis: Isaiah 58:1-11; Jeremiah 7:1-15; and Micah 6:1-8

Supplement: Legal Principles
The Point: The Old Testament law teaches us how to love God and other people.
Bible Basis: Exodus 20:1-17 and Leviticus 25:8-17, 39-46

P U B L I C I T Y   P A G E

Grab your congregation's attention! Add the vital details to the ready-made flier below, photocopy it, and use it to advertise this course on the Old Testament. Insert the flier in your bulletins. Enlarge it to make posters. Splash the art or anything else from this page in newsletters, in bulletins, or even on postcards! It's that simple.

The art from this page is available on Group's MinistryNet™ on-line resource. Call 800-447-1070 for more information.

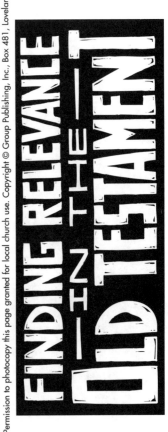

Compelling Stories

God is active in our world in various ways.

◀ THE POINT

OBJECTIVES

Participants will
- discuss how Old Testament stories shape their faith and their actions,
- learn how to read Old Testament stories with understanding, and
- discover the various ways God is active in Old Testament stories.

BIBLE BASIS

Look up the Scriptures for this lesson. Then read the following background paragraphs to see how the passages relate to people today.

The Old Testament stories weren't written simply to record history or to entertain their readers (though they often do both of those things). They were written to shape the thoughts and actions of the people who read them. Therefore, to understand a particular story, we must attempt to discover why that story was written the way that it was. Does the author wish to teach a theological truth concerning God, humanity, or the universe? Does the story portray behavior that we are to imitate or to avoid? As we carefully note *what* an author has included in terms of description, dialogue, and editorial explanation (you'll see these noted in the paragraphs that follow), we'll be better able to discover *why* the story was written and how we should apply it to our lives.

TEACHER TIP

To learn more about interpreting Hebrew narratives, read chapter 5 of *How to Read the Bible for All Its Worth*, by Gordon D. Fee and Douglas Stuart; chapters 2–3 of *How to Read the Bible as Literature*, by Leland Ryken; or chapters 3–7 of *The Art of Biblical Narrative*, by Robert Alter.

David didn't take the throne as soon as Samuel anointed him to be God's chosen king (1 Samuel 16:1-13). In fact, David had to endure numerous delays and even threats against his life before he began to rule. Still, the years of waiting weren't wasted. God used this time to teach David impor-

1 SAMUEL 26:1-25

tant theological and ethical truths. The author of 1 Samuel recounts David's experiences so God's people can learn and benefit from David's hard-earned lessons.

For example, 1 Samuel 26 depicts David as someone we should emulate [character description]. David agreed with Abishai that God had given Saul into his hand [dialogue—26:8, 23], but David rejected Abishai's evil impulse to assassinate God's anointed king. David also displayed moral superiority to Saul by refusing to kill even the one seeking to kill him. In the end, David could rightfully claim to be innocent, but Saul had to confess his guilt [dialogue—26:18-20, 21]. The narrator contrasts David with Saul and Abishai so we'll see in the character of David an ethical principle we're to follow. Like David, we should refuse to use evil means to achieve a good end, even when the good end is God's stated will (in David's case, to become king).

David could wait for God to make him king because he trusted God to protect and to reward him [dialogue—26:23-24]. The narrative supports David's expectation. Not only does Saul recognize that God would prosper David [dialogue—26:25], the narrator reveals that God was secretly protecting David all along [editorial explanation—26:12]. Interestingly enough, only God, the narrator, and the readers realize that God kept Saul and his army asleep during David's visit. This teaches us that God was active in David's situation even when David was unaware of it. Since God is also active in our situations whether we see it or not, we should follow David's example of avoiding every evil as we trust God to protect us and to accomplish his will for us.

2 CHRONICLES 20:1-30

In 2 Chronicles 20, the author reports that God transformed a foreign attack (20:1-4) into an occasion to bring riches and peace to his people and honor to himself (20:24-30). By contrasting an initial threat with its eventual reversal [situation description], the author teaches an important theological idea, namely, that God is always in control of the situation. As with David, God often works behind the scenes, but sometimes God acts in such a way that everyone can recognize his powerful and pervasive presence.

Against this background, Jehoshaphat (pronounced ji-hosh'-uh-fat) and the people of Judah appear as exemplars of faith and obedience [character description]. The author repeats three key words in both dialogue and descriptive sections to depict how Jehoshaphat and the people responded in this situation. They reacted to the threat by "standing" before the temple in Jerusalem (20:5, 9), which was the same as "standing" before God (20:13). They also obeyed when God told them to leave the safety of the temple and to "stand" before their attackers (20:17). Knowing that God was with them as they marched out before their enemies, they overcame their initial "fear" (20:3, 17) with "faith" in God and his prophetic word (20:20). Consequently, they enjoyed the victory that only God could bring.

For most Christians, the Old Testament narratives remain an untapped source of theological insight and ethical teaching. Although some may have a basic idea of *what* was written, few have reflected on *why* the stories were written. Use this lesson to help your class members read the Old Testament narratives with greater skill and confidence. In so doing, you'll increase their understanding and appreciation of an important part of God's Word.

THIS LESSON AT A GLANCE

Section	Minutes	What Participants Will Do	Supplies
OPENING	up to 10	**OLDIES BUT GOODIES**—Act out their favorite Old Testament stories and discuss why they should read all the Old Testament stories.	
BIBLE EXPLORATION AND APPLICATION	30 to 40	☐ *Option 1:* **CREATIVE ACTIVITY**—Move cotton balls to a goal and learn from 1 Samuel 26:1-25 and 2 Chronicles 20:1-30 that God uses various means to move people toward his goal.	Bibles, cotton balls, index cards, masking tape, paper, pencils, marker, newsprint
	25 to 35	☐ *Option 2:* **READ IT FOR YOURSELF**—Compare God's activity in the Bible to his activity in their lives, then learn how to read 1 Samuel 26:1-25 to discover that God is as active now as he was then.	Bibles, "Read It for Yourself" handouts (p. 25), pencils
CLOSING	up to 10	**YESTERDAY AND TODAY**—Describe how God has been active in their lives in the past and commit to responding to God's present activity in their lives.	Index cards, pencils
FOR EXTRA TIME	up to 15	**NOW YOU SEE IT, NOW YOU DON'T**—Compare the effects of presweetened drink mix and sugar on water to God's visible and invisible activity.	Cups, pitchers of water, presweetened drink mix, sugar, snacks
	up to 10	**MIRACLES: PAST AND PRESENT**—Define "miracle" and discuss the possibility and purpose of miracles today.	Newsprint, marker

Oldies but Goodies

(up to 10 minutes)

Form groups of four. Say: **Everyone likes a good story. That's probably why Old Testament stories such as Noah and the ark, David and Goliath, Daniel in the lions' den, and Moses at the Red Sea are popular with people of all ages and various religious backgrounds. Briefly tell your group members which Old Testament story is your favorite. Then, after everyone in your group names a favorite, choose one story to present to the rest of the class in a 60-second skit.**

Allow people two minutes to name their stories, then instruct groups to spend two minutes preparing their skits. When time is up, ask groups to take turns presenting their skits. Have groups not presenting the skit try to guess which story is being acted out.

After groups present their skits, invite people to call out favorite stories that weren't acted out. Then have group members discuss the following questions. After each question, ask for volunteers to report their groups' insights. Ask:

- **What do our favorite stories have in common? How are they different?**

- **Why do you prefer your favorite story to the other stories mentioned?**

- **What are the advantages of reading all the Old Testament stories?**

Say: **It's natural to be attracted to stories and characters we identify with, but each Old Testament story is a vital part of God's Word. Each one teaches us something important about God, our world, and ourselves. Today we're going to learn from the Old Testament that ▷God is active in our world in various ways.**

THE POINT ▷

☐ **OPTION 1:**

Creative Activity

(30 to 40 minutes)

Have each group of four divide into two pairs. Give each pair a cotton ball and two index cards. Use masking tape to mark starting and finish lines approximately 20 feet apart. Direct pairs to line up along the starting line and to set their cotton balls on the floor.

Say: **Following God's will for our lives is a lot like seeking to reach a goal. Let's have a race to illustrate what I mean. When I say "go," I want you and your partner to move your cotton ball from the starting line to your goal, which is the other side of the finish line. The pair that moves its cotton ball across the finish line first wins the race. Go!**

Encourage the class to applaud the winning pair, then ask the entire class the following questions:

- **What were the different methods people used to move the cotton balls?**

- **How did you feel when you saw pairs using methods different from yours?**

- **Which methods were most effective? Which were least effective?**

- **Why do you think I didn't limit the ways you could move the cotton balls?**

- **How is this like the way God moves us toward his goal? How is it different?**

Say: **Just as we could use different means to move the cotton balls to our goal, God can use different methods to move us toward his will or goal for our lives. He doesn't work the same way all the time. In fact, God's Word teaches that sometimes God uses radically different means to reach similar goals. To see what I mean, let's briefly examine two Old Testament stories, one about King David and the other about King Jehoshaphat** (pronounced ji-hosh´-uh-fat).

Assign **1 Samuel 26:1-25** to half of the pairs and **2 Chronicles 20:1-30** to the other half. Have each pair join another pair with the same biblical text to form a group of four. Give each person a sheet of paper and a pencil. Instruct group members to read their assigned biblical passages.

While people are reading, write the following instructions on a sheet of newsprint and hang it where everyone can see it:
- Summarize what happened in three to four sentences.
- List the different ways God was active in your story.
- Describe how the people responded to God's activity.

When groups finish reading, have them spend eight minutes completing the instructions for their passages. Then have each pair join another pair with the other biblical text to form a new group of four. Direct the two pairs within each group of four to teach each other what they learned about their passages.

After five minutes, have group members discuss the fol-

TEACHER TIP

It's important not to tell people how they may or may not move the cotton balls. Some pairs may fan the cotton balls with the index cards, while others may carry the cotton balls on the cards. Still others may pick up the cotton balls with their hands and carry them across the finish line. To illustrate how God uses different means to move us to his goal, allow pairs to use any method that's safe to everyone present.

lowing questions. After each question, ask for volunteers to report their groups' insights to the rest of the class. Ask:

- **In what ways was the level of God's activity the same? different?**

- **How was the people's awareness of God's activity the same? different?**

- **What do these passages teach about the ways God is active in our world?**

- **What do they teach about how we should respond to God's activity?**

Say: **Because ▶God is active in our world in *various* ways, we must not assume that he'll work in our lives as he works in others' lives or even that he'll always work in our lives in exactly the same way. The one thing we know for certain is that he *is* active. What we can't know for sure is *how* God is active in our lives or our world.**

Instruct people to discuss the following questions within their original pairs. Ask:

- **How do you think God is active in your life right now?**

- **What do you think the goal of God's activity might be?**

- **How should you respond to God's activity in your life?**

Encourage people to write down their answers to the prior question. Then instruct partners to pray, asking God to make them more aware of and responsive to his activity in their lives.

■■■■■■■■■■■■■■■■■■■■■■■■■

FOR *Even Deeper* DISCUSSION

Form groups of four to discuss the following questions:

- Why do you think God sometimes keeps his activity hidden? sometimes acts openly? How might God strengthen our faith by working openly? by working behind the scenes?

- Read Genesis 2:1-3. To what extent does God's "rest" involve inactivity? To what extent does it signal a change in the way God is active? What does this teach about the way God's activity changes to meet new situations?

■■■■■■■■■■■■■■■■■■■■■■■■■

☐ **OPTION 2:**
Read It for Yourself
(25 to 35 minutes)

Before class, make one photocopy of the "Read It for Yourself" handout (p. 25) for each class member.

Keep people in their groups of four from the Opening. Have group members discuss the following questions. After each question, ask for volunteers to report their groups' answers to the rest of the class. Ask:

- **On a scale of 0 to 10, with 0 being inactive and 10 being very active, how active was God in your favorite story? Explain.**

- **Now, using the same scale of 0 to 10, how active was God in your life this past week? Explain.**

- **To what extent are the levels of God's activity in your story and your life the same? different?**

- **How are the evidences of God's activity in your favorite story and your life the same? different?**

Say: **It's not unusual to feel that God works differently today than he did during Old Testament times. Even though we know that God never changes, we may feel, at times, that God acts differently today than he did back then. The best response to those feelings is to go to God's Word to find out how things really were and are. Instead of asking other people what they think, we should go directly to the source to discover what God has said. Of course, to do that, we need to know how to read and understand the Bible for ourselves. So let's spend the next few minutes learning how to read the Old Testament stories with insight and understanding.**

Give everyone a copy of the "Read It for Yourself" handout and a pencil. Instruct group members to read and to follow the instructions at the top of the handout.

After 10 minutes, ask for volunteers to report what they discovered to the rest of the class. Then ask the entire class the following questions:

- **What does this story teach us about God's involvement in the world?**

- **What does it teach about how we should respond to God's activity?**

Then have people discuss the following questions within their groups:

- **How is God's activity in your life like God's activity in the story? How is it different?**

- **How should you avoid acting as Saul did? imitate David's response to God's activity?**

Say: **If we weren't able to read and understand the Bible for ourselves, we might think that God isn't as involved in our lives as he was in the lives of biblical characters. But by carefully reading 1 Samuel 25, we discovered that ▶ God is active in our world in various**

**BIBLE**
I N S I G H T

David had already spared Saul's life one time (1 Samuel 24:1-15). On that occasion David felt remorse for secretly cutting off the corner of Saul's royal robe, which was apparently a symbolic attack on Saul himself. This time David took Saul's spear and water jar, presumably for different reasons. David probably took the spear to show that he meant Saul no harm and then returned the spear so Saul would have the ability to defend himself. David may have kept the water jar, however, to symbolically limit Saul's ability to continue chasing him into the wilderness.

◀ **T H E   P O I N T**

ways, even when we're not aware of it. And just as we uncovered this truth by examining God's Word for ourselves, we can discover other important truths by applying the same principles of interpretation that we used today to other Old Testament stories.

■ ■

FOR *Even Deeper* DISCUSSION

Form groups of four to discuss the following questions:
● When, if ever, might God choose to be inactive for a period of time? When might God take his hands off a situation? leave us to our own devices? let us wait?
● What should we do if God seems to be inactive? if we don't know how God is being active? How can we know if we should wait for a miracle? take matters into our own hands?

■ ■

Apply·It·To·Life™ The "Apply-It-To-Life This Week!" hand-
This Week! out (p. 26) helps people further explore the issues uncovered in today's class. Give everyone a photocopy of the handout. Encourage class members to take time during the coming week to explore the questions and activities on the handout.

CLOSING

Yesterday and Today

(up to 10 minutes)

Have people remain in (or re-form) groups of four from the Opening. Say: **In Malachi 3:6, God declares, "I the Lord do not change." Because God never changes, we can be certain that he is as active in our world as he was in the world of the Old Testament. Sometimes we simply need to look more closely for signs of his presence and activity.**

Give each person an index card and a pencil. Tell each person to write on the card one way God has been active in his or her life in the past. After one minute, have group members tell each other what they've written.

After everyone has shared, instruct each person to write on the card one way he or she will respond to God's activity today. For example, someone might write, "Try to discover what God is doing in my life," while someone else might write, "Follow God's leading regarding my job." After one minute, have group members share what they wrote with each other.

Then have group members close in prayer, thanking God for his involvement in their lives in the past and asking God to help them recognize and properly respond to his involvement in their lives today.

When people finish praying, say: **The Old Testament teaches that ▶ God is active in our world and in our lives in various ways. Keep your card as a reminder that God has been and will be active in your life at all times. Then commit to looking for and responding to God's activity no matter what your situation might be.**

◀ T H E   P O I N T

 For Extra Time

NOW YOU SEE IT, NOW YOU DON'T
(up to 15 minutes)

Set out two small cups for each class member and two clear pitchers of water. Mix a pack of presweetened drink mix into one of the pitchers and one cup of sugar into the other. Then invite class members to sample both drinks. After everyone has tasted both drinks, set out several plates of cut fruit, crackers, or cookies for people to enjoy with their drinks.

Then form groups of four to discuss the following questions:

- **How was the action of the drink mix like that of the sugar? How was it different?**

- **How is this similar to the way God is active in our lives? How is it different?**

- **When has God been visibly active in your life? invisibly active?**

- **How should we respond to the knowledge that God is always active in our lives?**

MIRACLES: PAST AND PRESENT
(up to 10 minutes)

Hang a sheet of newsprint where everyone can see it. Then ask the entire class to suggest a definition of "miracle." Record people's suggestions on the newsprint. When everyone agrees on the general meaning of the word, ask people for examples of biblical miracles. Then form groups of four to discuss the following questions:

- **To what extent does God perform miracles today?**

- **What was the purpose of the biblical miracles?**

- What might be God's purpose for miracles today?
- How might we recognize miracles when they happen?

Read It for Yourself

Learn to interpret Old Testament stories for yourself. Read the FYI box below and 1 Samuel 26:1-25. Then answer the questions below. You have 10 minutes to complete the handout

FOR YOUR INFORMATION

We interpret biblical stories by discovering why they were written the way they were. Are we to learn a theological truth about God, ourselves, or our world? Does the story portray behavior we are to imitate or to avoid? As we carefully note *what* an author included in terms of description, dialogue, and editorial explanation, we can discover *why* a story was written and how we should apply it to our lives.

DESCRIPTION

● How does the author portray David's situation? David's reaction to his situation?

● What are we to learn from Saul's negative behavior? David's positive behavior?

DIALOGUE

● How are Abishai's (verse 8) and David's (verse 23) reactions similar? different?

● What ethical principle does the author teach by contrasting David with Abishai?

EXPLANATION

● What does the report of verse 12 add to our understanding of what happened?

● What does this explanation teach about God's activity? about our awareness of it?

Apply·It·To·Life™
This Week!

Compelling Stories

God is active in our world in various ways.
**1 Samuel 26:1-25 and
2 Chronicles 20:1-30**

Reflecting on God's Word

Each day this week, read one of the following Scriptures and examine what it teaches about different ways God is active in our world. Then consider how you can recognize and respond to God's activity in your life. List your discoveries in the space under each passage.

Day 1: Ruth 1:1-22. Ruth and Naomi return to Judah.

Day 2: Ruth 2:1-23. Ruth gleans in the field of Boaz.

Day 3: Ruth 3:1-18. Boaz promises to marry Ruth.

Day 4: Ruth 4:1-22. Ruth and Boaz wed and have a son.

Day 5: Daniel 1:1-21. Daniel refuses the king's food.

Day 6: Daniel 6:1-28. God saves Daniel from the lions.

Beyond Reflection

Create a journal in which you record God's active presence in your life. At the end of each day, list one way God was visibly active in your work, home, or relationships with others and one way God may have been secretly active in the same areas. Then think about how you responded to God's activity and how you might have acted even better. Finally, thank God for his active presence in your life, and ask God to help you respond to his activity in appropriate ways.

Coming Next Week: Honest Prayers
(Psalms 13:1-6; 16:1-11; 63:1-11; and 103:1-22)

Honest Prayers

God always wants us to tell him exactly how we feel.

OBJECTIVES

Participants will
- discover why and how they should express themselves to God,
- learn to interpret several types of Old Testament psalms, and
- express their thoughts and feelings to God in a biblical way.

BIBLE BASIS

Look up the Scriptures for this lesson. Then read the following background paragraphs to see how the passages relate to people today.

The psalms of the Old Testament contributed greatly to the worship and the theology of ancient Israel. Properly utilized, they perform a similarly important function in the life of the modern church. For example, reading the psalms as paradigms or models of prayer shows us how to talk to God in every circumstance or state of mind. In addition, examining them as sources of theological truth enriches our understanding of God and our own situations. Finally, reciting them during times of personal and public worship deepens our relationship with and our appreciation for God.

When we read the psalms, we should keep in mind at least two interpretive principles. First, the Old Testament contains different kinds of psalms, each with its own intention or aim. Some psalms seek God's intervention, others his exaltation. Therefore, one goal of interpretation should be to identify both the psalm's type and what it hopes to achieve. Second, the psalms are poetry. As such, they use language that is more emotional than analytical, more expressive than objective. Consequently, we should read and appropriate the psalms as poetic prayers that express acceptable human feelings to God and authentic human longings for his involvement in our lives.

TEACHER **TIP**

To learn more about reading and appropriating the psalms for today, consult *The Message of the Psalms*, by Walter Brueggemann; *Interpreting the Psalms*, by Patrick D. Miller Jr.; or chapter 11 of *How to Read the Bible for All Its Worth*, by Gordon D. Fee and Douglas Stuart.

PSALM 13:1-6   Psalm 13 provides a classic example of a petitionary prayer or complaint psalm. It begins with a series of rhetorical questions that express the psalmist's perception of his situation and his belief that the situation has continued for too long. Verses 3 and 4 shift the focus to the psalm's main intention, which is to persuade God to provide healing. Finally, the psalm concludes with a confident affirmation that God will answer the prayer and intervene in the situation.

As a model for prayer, Psalm 13 shows us how to respond when life is bad. First, we should express in clear and direct terms how we feel and what we'd like God to do about it. Above all else, prayers of complaint must be honest. Second, complaint is not an end in and of itself. Rather, it enables us to articulate our feelings and to place our longings before God as the only one who can make a difference in our situation. In this way, complaint becomes an expression of faith in the power and the goodness of God.

PSALMS 16:1-11 AND 63:1-11   Psalms 16 and 63 resemble Psalm 13 in several important respects. In these psalms, however, the complaint is so muted (16:1) and the expressions of faith so pronounced that one should classify them psalms of trust, not psalms of complaint. Psalms of confidence or trust generally contain at least two elements: confessions of faith and expressions of confidence. The confessions of faith assure God of the psalmist's devotion (16:2, 5; 63:1, 8), while the expressions of confidence remind the psalmist of the benefits of being devoted to God (16:5-11; 63:7, 8b, 9-10).

When we read psalms of this type, we should seek to uncover the details of and the reasons for the psalmist's confidence in God. In so doing, we discover both what we can trust God to do and why we can trust him to do it. Finally, we also learn from these psalms how to express and to increase our confidence in God. During times of crisis, such confidence enables us to complain to God as an act of faith instead of an expression of frustration.

PSALM 103:1-22   When most people think of the book of Psalms, they think of psalms of praise or hymns such as Psalm 103. This psalm begins and ends with a call to praise God (103:1-2, 20-22). In between, the psalmist offers reasons God is worthy of praise. Instead of "repaying" us according to our sins (103:10, see 8-12), God "repays" us with spiritual and physical benefits (Hebrew "repays" = English "benefits"—103:2, see 3-5). In addition, although we are as insubstantial as dust and grass (103:13-16), God's parental compassion and loyal love for us will endure forever (103:8, 13, 17-18).

The Old Testament hymns contribute to the lives of God's people in several ways. They help us worship God in a meaningful and appropriate manner, and they instruct us concerning God's character and activity in our lives. By way of example, they also teach us to praise God for who he is *and* for what he does. Because God's character determines his actions and his actions reveal his character, the two cannot be separated.

The Old Testament contains psalms of different types to meet various situations and needs. Taken together, the psalms show us how to talk to God in every situation of life. That is, the psalms teach us how to express our complaints to God when life is bad. However, we should do so as an act of confidence in God's power and goodness. Then, when God answers our petitions, we should respond to him with thanksgiving and praise. Use this lesson to help your class talk to God honestly and appropriately no matter how good or how bad their situation might be.

THIS LESSON AT A GLANCE

Section	Minutes	What Participants Will Do	Supplies
OPENING	*up to 10*	**EXPRESS YOURSELF**—Pantomime emotions and discuss how words enable them to express their emotions clearly.	Index cards, pencil
BIBLE EXPLORATION AND APPLICATION	*25 to 35*	☐ *Option 1:* **TELL IT TO GOD**—Express and discuss negative emotions, then study Psalm 13 to learn how to properly express negative emotions to God.	Bibles, paper, markers, tape, scissors, index cards, pencils, construction paper, newsprint
	30 to 40	☐ *Option 2:* **A PSALM FOR EVERY OCCASION**—Write their own psalms; study Psalms 13, 16, 63, and 103; and revise their psalms to be more like the biblical ones.	Bibles, "A Psalm for Every Occasion" handouts (p. 36), pencils, paper
CLOSING	*up to 10*	**LETTERS TO GOD**—Write letters telling God how they feel and commit to being more open and honest with God.	Paper, pencils
FOR EXTRA TIME	*up to 10*	**REAL EMOTIONS, REAL PRAYERS**—Role play expressing positive and negative feelings to God.	Newsprint, marker, tape
	up to 10	**PRACTICE MAKES PERFECT**—Interpret more psalms of praise, trust, and complaint.	Bibles, marker, newsprint, tape

Express Yourself

(up to 10 minutes)

Before class, write the following words on separate index cards: anger, hope, fear, despair, confidence, confusion, adoration, joy. Make enough cards, repeating the words as necessary, so each class member will have one.

As people arrive, hand each person a card. Tell people to keep secret what is written on their cards. Then form groups of four. Instruct group members to pantomime the emotions written on their cards. While one person silently acts out an emotion, other group members are to guess which emotion is being represented. If people don't guess the emotion within one minute, have the person tell what the emotion is.

When everyone has finished acting out an emotion, have group members discuss the following questions. After each question, ask for volunteers to report their answers to the rest of the class. Ask:

- **How did it feel to express your emotion without using words?**

- **How effectively were you able to communicate your emotion?**

- **How could you have expressed your emotion more effectively?**

- **How is this like the way you express your emotions to God? How is it different?**

Say: **It's hard to express our emotions when we don't have the freedom or the ability to put those feelings into words. And it's difficult to have a close relationship with someone when we can't tell that person what we're feeling. But today we'll discover that we have the freedom and the ability to draw close to God because** ▷**God always wants us to tell him exactly how we feel.**

T H E   P O I N T ▷

BIBLE **E**XPLORATION
AND **A**PPLICATION

☐ **O**PTION **1:**

Tell It to God

(25 to 35 minutes)

Set out the following supplies: paper, markers, tape, scissors, index cards, pencils, and construction paper.

Tell people to think of a negative emotion—for example, anger, hate, fear, resentment, or hurt—they have toward a spouse, parent, child, friend, or co-worker. Pause a few seconds, then say: **Without revealing the identity of the person you're thinking of, use the supplies I've set out to express your feelings toward that person. For example, you can write a poem, a letter, a limerick, or a song. You may even want to create a poster to express your feelings. Choose whatever form you're most comfortable with. In five minutes, you'll share what you've created with a partner... other than your spouse.**

When time is up, have everyone choose a partner other than a spouse. Ask partners to briefly share what they wrote. When pairs finish, give people the opportunity to share what they wrote with the entire class. Then have pairs discuss the following questions. Ask:

- **How did it feel to express your negative emotion in a concrete way?**

- **What are the benefits of expressing that emotion? What are the drawbacks?**

- **What would happen if you told the person you wrote about how you feel?**

- **How would God react if you told him you had negative feelings about him?**

Say: **Life would be easy if we always felt good about everyone and everything. However, we all experience negative emotions from time to time, so we all need to learn how to deal with them in the proper way. Fortunately, God shows us in the book of Psalms how we can express every emotion, even negative ones we may have toward him, in a healthy and appropriate way.**

Have each pair join another pair to form a group of four. Instruct groups to read **Psalm 13:1-6.** While groups are reading, write the following questions on a sheet of newsprint and hang it where everyone can see it:

- What emotions is the psalmist experiencing?

- What is the apparent cause of those feelings?

- How does the psalmist deal with his feelings?

- What's the result of dealing with those feelings?

Instruct group members to spend eight minutes answering the questions. When time is up, ask for volunteers to report their groups' answers to each question. Then ask the entire class the following questions:

- **What does this psalm teach us about how to express negative emotions?**

BIBLE INSIGHT

The repetition of three words in Psalm 13 shows how the psalmist's complaint is overcome and reversed by his confidence in God. First, although the psalmist addresses God simply as "Lord" in the complaint, he has the faith to make his appeal to the "Lord *my* God" (verse 3). In addition, although the psalmist has sorrow in his "heart" (verse 2) because his foes will "rejoice" at his dilemma (verse 4), he trusts that his "heart" will "rejoice" in God's salvation (verse 5).

● What does the psalm teach about the benefits of telling God how we feel?

Then have people re-form their original pairs and discuss the following questions with their partners. Ask:

● How can you express to God the emotion you wrote about earlier?

● What will be the likely benefits of expressing that emotion to God?

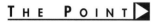THE POINT▷

Say: **It's fairly obvious that God loves to hear our praises, but God also wants us to tell him our hurts, fears, and complaints. In fact, the book of Psalms teaches that ▷God always wants to hear exactly how we feel. As we read and follow the example of the biblical psalms, we'll have both the confidence and the ability to talk to God no matter what our situation or state of mind.**

■■■■■■■■■■■■■■■■■■■■■■■■■

FOR *Even Deeper* DISCUSSION

Form groups of four to discuss the following questions:

● To what extent should we tell God how we feel about others? about him? To what extent should we tell others how we feel about them? about God?

● Read Mark 3:28-30. What does it mean to blaspheme against the Holy Spirit? How might Jesus' warning influence or limit what we express to God? how we express our feelings to God?

■■■■■■■■■■■■■■■■■■■■■■■■■

□ **OPTION 2:**

A Psalm for Every Occasion

(30 to 40 minutes)

Before class, make one photocopy of the "Psalm for Every Occasion" handout (p. 36) for each class member.

Keep people in their groups of four from the Opening. Give each group a sheet of paper and a pencil. Say: **One of the most effective ways to learn how to do something is to actually do it. So the best way for us to learn about psalms is to write one. With that in mind, I want you to work with your group members to write a psalm. Spend one minute talking about what you'd like to say to God, then have each group member write two lines of the psalm. You have five minutes to discuss**

and write your psalm.

When time is up, ask a representative from each group to read the psalm. Then have group members discuss the following questions. After each question, ask for volunteers to report their groups' answers. Ask:

- **In what ways are the psalms we wrote similar? different?**

- **What emotions and feelings were expressed by our psalms?**

- **What does this reveal about our understanding of psalms?**

- **What does it say about how we think we should talk to God?**

Say: **It's not unusual for people to think that God only wants to hear pleasant prayers and positive feelings. But the book of Psalms contains a variety of prayers that express various human emotions. Let's examine some of those psalms to discover not only what we can say to God but also how we should say it.**

Give a copy of the "Psalm for Every Occasion" handout to each person and a pencil to anyone who needs one. Assign each group one of the following **Psalms: 13; 16; 63; 103.** Tell group members to read and follow the instructions at the top of the handout.

After five minutes, ask groups to report what they discovered about their psalms. Encourage people to fill in the handout sections they didn't complete within their groups. When every group has reported, ask the entire class the following questions:

- **What do these psalms teach about which emotions we can express to God?**

- **What do the psalms teach about how we should complain to God? praise God?**

- **In what ways are the biblical psalms and those we wrote alike? different?**

- **How might we change our psalms to make them more like the biblical psalms?**

Tell groups to spend three minutes revising their psalms so they are more like the biblical psalms. Then have groups read their revised psalms.

Say: **Many people assume that every psalm is a hymn and that God only wants to hear our words of praise. But the book of Psalms shows us that ▶God always wants to hear exactly how we feel. Since there is a psalm for every occasion and situation of life, we should read the book of Psalms regularly to learn how to express our every emotion to God in an honest and appropriate way.**

TEACHER TIP

If you have fewer than four groups, assign two psalms to each group and increase the study time to 10 minutes. If you decide not to use all four psalms, omit Psalm 63 first and Psalm 16 second.

BIBLE INSIGHT

Hymns, complaints, and psalms of trust are the most common types of psalms, but the Bible also includes royal psalms (2; 72; 110), thanksgiving psalms (30; 32; 34), wisdom psalms (37; 49; 73), liturgies (15; 132), and even a wedding psalm (45). Given the wide range of topics discussed and emotions expressed in Psalms, one can legitimately conclude that there is truly a psalm for every occasion.

◀ THE POINT

FOR *Even Deeper* DISCUSSION

Form groups of four to discuss the following questions:

● How can expressing negative feelings to God help us overcome those feelings? How might expressing confidence in God increase our confidence in him?

● What are the crucial elements of biblical praise? How does authentic praise affect God? the one praising? How might we use praise to encourage others? to teach others?

■ ■

 The "Apply-It-To-Life This Week!" handout (p. 37) helps people further explore the issues uncovered in today's class. Give everyone a photocopy of the handout. Encourage class members to take time during the coming week to explore the questions and activities on the handout.

CLOSING

Letters to God

(up to 10 minutes)

THE POINT ▷

Say: **Knowing that ▷God always wants us to tell him how we feel won't mean much if we don't actually tell God how we feel. So let's close today's lesson by spending a few minutes honestly telling God what's on our hearts and minds right now.**

Give a sheet of paper to each person and a pencil to anyone who needs one. Instruct people to spend five minutes alone writing a letter to God. Encourage people to be completely honest and open in what they write by assuring them that no one else will see the letter.

After five minutes, get everyone's attention. Instruct people to silently answer the following questions. Pause 30 to 60 seconds after each question. Ask:

● **How might telling God how you feel improve your relationship with God?**

● **What will you do to ensure you always tell God exactly how you feel?**

THE POINT ▷

Say: **Since ▷God always wants to hear exactly how we feel, we need to be sure that we're always open and honest with him. Take home your letter and read it to God before you go to bed tonight. Then use the letter as a reminder to tell God what's on your heart and mind every day.**

TEACHER TIP

If class members would like to learn more about praying honestly, follow up this course on the Old Testament with the Apply-It-To-Life course titled *Honest to God: Prayer for Every Day.*

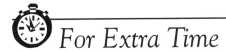

For Extra Time

REAL EMOTIONS, REAL PRAYERS
(up to 10 minutes)

Form pairs. Write the following situations on a sheet of newsprint and hang it where everyone can see it:

- Your child has been diagnosed with cancer.
- You're living alone for the first time ever.
- You've been forced to declare bankruptcy.
- Your boss gave you an unexpected pay raise.
- God granted your pleas to heal your friend.
- Your runaway child just came back home.

Have each person choose one of the first three situations and think about how he or she would feel if faced with that situation. Then have partners practice telling God what they would feel by taking turns expressing those feelings to each other. Have listening partners affirm their partners for what they did well and suggest ways they might express their feelings better.

After three minutes, have each person choose one of the last three situations and repeat the process. Then ask the entire class the following questions:

- **How easily were you able to express what you might feel?**

- **What can you do to express yourself to God more freely?**

PRACTICE MAKES PERFECT
(up to 10 minutes)

To help class members gain confidence and skill interpreting psalms, have them study additional psalms of praise (8; 100; 111; 113), trust (11; 23; 27; 62), and complaint (5; 7; 26; 142). Form groups of four and assign one psalm to each group. While groups are reading their psalms, write the following questions on a sheet of newsprint and hang it where everyone can see it:

- Is your psalm a hymn, a psalm of confidence, or a complaint?
- What does the psalmist hope to accomplish with the psalm?
- What does the psalm teach about how we should talk to God?
- How can we apply the psalm's example to our prayer lives?

Direct groups to answer the questions for their psalms. After five minutes, ask for volunteers to report their groups' insights to the rest of the class. If time permits, have groups read and interpret another set of psalms.

TEACHER **TIP**

If you didn't complete Option 2, read students the information in the FYI box on the "Psalm for Every Occasion" handout (p. 36) before you have them answer the questions.

A *Psalm* • FOR EVERY OCCASION •

$\mathcal{R}$ead the information in the FYI box and your assigned psalm. Then fill in the blanks for your psalm. In five minutes, you'll report your conclusions to the rest of the class.

FOR **Y**OUR **■**NFORMATION

Because there are different kinds of psalms, each with its own intention or aim, one goal of interpretation is to identify the psalm's type and what it hopes to achieve. *Complaints* seek God's intervention; *hymns,* God's exaltation; while *psalms of trust* express the psalmist's confidence in and commitment to God. In addition, since psalms use poetic language that is more emotional than analytical and more expressive than objective, we should read the psalms as poetic prayers that express acceptable human feelings to God.

Psalm 13	*Psalm 16*
TYPE	TYPE
GOAL	GOAL
FEELINGS ABOUT GOD	FEELINGS ABOUT GOD
Psalm 63	*Psalm 103*
TYPE	TYPE
GOAL	GOAL
FEELINGS ABOUT GOD	FEELINGS ABOUT GOD

Apply·It·To·Life™ This Week!

Honest Prayers

God always wants us to tell
him exactly how we feel.
**Psalms 13:1-6; 16:1-11;
63:1-11; and 103:1-22**

Reflecting on God's Word

Each day this week, read one of the following psalms and examine how the psalmist talks to God and others. Then consider how you can follow the psalmist's example in your own prayer life. List your discoveries in the space under each passage.

Day 1: Psalm 8:1-9. The majesty of creation is reason to praise God.

Day 2: Psalm 23:1-6. We can rest confidently in God's care for us.

Day 3: Psalm 40:1-17. God wants us to thank him and ask him for help.

Day 4: Psalm 62:1-12. We should patiently wait for God to help us.

Day 5: Psalm 130:1-8. We can approach God because he forgives our sins.

Day 6: Psalm 139:1-24. Nothing we do or say is hidden from God.

Beyond Reflection

All too often our prayers are vague and lifeless. To infuse your prayer life with life and clarity, write a letter to God at least once a week. In the letter, talk honestly about the problems you're facing, how you feel about those problems, and how you'd like God to help you solve your problems. In addition, list everything good God has done for you during the week, then thank and praise God for his specific acts of kindness. Periodically review the letters for insight into God's activity in your life.

Coming Next Week: True Wisdom
(Proverbs 1:1-7; 24:30-34; and Ecclesiastes 5:18-20; 12:13-14)

True Wisdom

God gave us our minds, and he expects us to use them.

◀ **THE POINT**

OBJECTIVES

Participants will
- discover that God reveals truth through a variety of means,
- recognize their responsibility to think for themselves, and
- learn how to discover truth in God's Word and in God's world.

BIBLE BASIS

Look up the Scriptures for this lesson. Then read the following background paragraphs to see how the passages relate to people today.

The Old Testament books of Job, Proverbs, and Ecclesiastes represent the pinnacle of Israelite wisdom and present a pattern for becoming wise. To understand and to use these books as they were intended, we should keep at least three principles in mind as we mine their riches.

First, conclusions are stated in general rather than absolute terms. So, although biblical proverbs are always true, they're not always relevant. To be wise, one must know both what is true and which truths apply in a given situation (see Proverbs 24:5-6). Second, Israelite wisdom derives from human observation and reflection, not from direct divine revelation. Since the Israelite sages based their conclusions on what they saw and not on what God said, we are free to test their ideas against our own observations and experiences. Finally, the goal of wisdom is skillful and successful living. The wisdom books focus more on practical realities than on abstract reasonings, so we should read them to learn how to live responsibly before God and joyfully in his world.

Although these verses were originally written to introduce the book of Proverbs, they also outline several key assumptions of the Israelite wisdom tradition. First, the source and

TEACHER
TIP

To learn more about Old Testament wisdom literature, read chapter 12 of *How to Read the Bible for All Its Worth*, by Gordon D. Fee and Douglas Stuart; chapter 6 of *How to Read the Bible as Literature*, by Leland Ryken; or *What Are They Saying About Wisdom Literature?* by Dianne Bergant.

PROVERBS 1:1-7

the goal of true wisdom is God (verse 7). All truth derives from him (Proverbs 8:1, 22-31), and the chief end of wisdom is a right relationship with him. Moreover, wisdom is more a moral quality than an intellectual quest. Therefore, the truly wise will have lives filled with "righteousness, justice, and equity" (1:3) and not just heads filled with facts. Finally, since wisdom is not just intellectual but also spiritual and moral, it is available to the simple and the wise alike (verses 4-5). True wisdom isn't reserved for the intellectual elite; it is available and accessible to anyone who honestly searches for it.

PROVERBS 24:30-34   From these few verses the observant reader can derive both an important piece of practical advice and a clear example of the best way to become wise. In the first place, this text teaches by way of example that people who "lack" sense (verse 30) will end up "lacking" (verse 34) the things they need. Simply put, people who are lazy should expect to be poor as well.

In addition to teaching this helpful lesson, these verses also describe the "wisdom method" in action. The first step is to carefully *observe* the people and situations we encounter (verses 30-31). Then, by *reflecting* on what we have observed, we can discover the lessons that every encounter contains (verse 32). Finally, to help us remember what we've learned and to enable us to teach it to others, we should *record* the lesson in a memorable proverb or saying (verses 33-34). As we follow this method, we'll be able to discover lessons just as true and helpful as the one taught by these verses.

ECCLESIASTES 5:18-20   Although scholars often characterize Ecclesiastes as cynical and pessimistic, the book is actually quite practical and realistic. In these verses, for example, we find both an honest view of the nature of life and some helpful advice on enjoying life regardless of our circumstances.

The Teacher (see 1:1) admits that everyone must "labor" or "toil" in life (5:18-19) and that, although God enables some people to enjoy the riches of their toil, God also allows some to live in poverty. Since, therefore, we must labor with no guarantee of success, we should find whatever enjoyment we can in our labor (verse 18) and enjoy whatever prosperity God brings our way (verse 19).

ECCLESIASTES 12:13-14   If our *only* goal is to enjoy life as fully as possible, however, we'll inevitably neglect our responsibilities to God and to others. Wisdom suggests a more balanced approach. As we enjoy each moment, we must remember that God sees everything we do and will judge us according to our deeds (verse 14). Knowing this, the wise person balances enjoyment of life with reverence for God (verse 13). If we are wise, we will obey God's commands *and* enjoy his benefits. In so doing, we will honor God and enrich ourselves in the best possible way.

At times people feel as though they must leave their minds at the door when they walk into church. However, the Old Testament wisdom books completely refute this attitude. Because God gave us our minds, he expects us to use them to their fullest extent to learn how to live responsibly before him and enjoyably with others. Use this lesson to help your students discover their ability and their responsibility to honor God and benefit themselves through the proper use of their God-given minds.

THIS LESSON AT A GLANCE

Section	Minutes	What Participants Will Do	Supplies
OPENING	*up to 10*	**PROVERBIAL WISDOM**—Compare favorite sayings to biblical proverbs to learn that God has revealed truth in various ways.	Bible, marker, newsprint, tape
BIBLE EXPLORATION AND APPLICATION	*25 to 35*	☐ *Option 1:* **FEEDING OURSELVES**—Compete in eating races, then study Proverbs 1:1-7; 24:30-34; and Ecclesiastes 5:18-20; 12:13-14 to discover how and why they should feed themselves mentally.	Bibles, plates of rice cereal, forks, marker, newsprint, tape, paper, pencils
	30 to 40	☐ *Option 2:* **WALKING IN WISDOM**—Practice the wisdom method of Proverbs 24:30-34 by walking outside and by comparing what they learn outside to what they learn in Ecclesiastes 5:18-20 and 12:13-14.	Bibles, pencils, index cards, paper
CLOSING	*up to 10*	**BOTH SIDES OF THE STORY**—Compare an index card to God's wisdom and commit to seeking biblical and general wisdom.	Newsprint, tape, marker, index cards, pencils
FOR EXTRA TIME	*up to 10*	**TRUTH FOR TODAY**—Discuss both sides of a current issue to discover how to form wise opinions today.	Paper, pencils

Proverbial Wisdom

(up to 10 minutes)

Before class, write the words of the following verses on a sheet of newsprint: **Proverbs 10:18; 15:1; 16:18;** and **27:5.**

Form groups of four, and have people tell their group members their favorite sayings or maxims. For example, someone might contribute, "A stitch in time saves nine" or "If a job is worth doing, it's worth doing well."

While groups are sharing, hang a blank sheet of newsprint where everyone can see it. After two minutes, have people call out some of their favorite sayings. As people call out sayings, write them on the sheet of newsprint.

When you have five or six sayings, read each one aloud, asking everyone who believes the saying is true to raise a hand. Record the number of votes in favor of each saying on the newsprint. After people vote on all the sayings, hang the newsprint with the biblical proverbs, and repeat the process.

Then have group members discuss the following questions. Ask for volunteers to report their groups' responses after each question. Ask:

- **How are the folk sayings and proverbs alike? different?**

- **Why do you believe the biblical proverbs are true?**

- **How can you determine if a folk saying is true or not?**

Say: **When we say that the Bible is true, we're not implying that everything outside of the Bible is necessarily false. The Bible itself teaches us to look for God's truth in various places. So today we'll examine the Old Testament wisdom books to discover**

T H E   P O I N T ▷ **why ▷ God gave us our minds and how he expects us to use them.**

☐ **OPTION 1:**

Feeding Ourselves

(25 to 35 minutes)

Set out one paper plate for every two class members. Pour one-half cup of Rice Krispies or similar cereal on each plate. Set out one fork for every two people.

Keep people in their groups of four. Instruct group members to number off by fours. Say: **Before we turn our attention to the Bible, I want each group to race to see who can eat a plate of cereal the fastest. In a minute, I'll have each two and each three come and get one plate and one fork. When they return to their groups, they can start the race. Here are your race instructions: Number one, feed number two; number three, feed yourself; number four, time the race and assess any penalties. (For example, one second will be added to your time for each piece of cereal dropped.) And, finally, number four, declare the winner. Any questions?** Pause. **Twos and threes, come get your cereal.**

When all races are finished, ask the fours to report whether the teams or the individuals won. Then have group members discuss the following questions. Ask:

- **What emotions did you experience during your competition?**

- **Why is feeding ourselves generally better than being fed by others?**

- **How is relying on others to feed our minds like depending on others to feed our bodies? How is it different?**

- **In what ways do we rely on others to feed us intellectually or spiritually?**

Say: **We generally expect 10-year-old children to know how to feed themselves, but it's not uncommon for 10-year-old Christians to rely on others for spiritual and intellectual food. However, Old Testament wisdom books, such as Job, Proverbs, and Ecclesiastes, teach that ▷ God gave us our minds, and he expects us to use them. Let's examine two passages in Proverbs to see exactly what God wants us to do.**

Assign **Proverbs 1:1-7** to half the groups and **Proverbs 24:30-34** to the other half. Give each group a sheet of paper and a pencil. Instruct group members to read their passages. While groups are reading, write the following questions on a sheet of newsprint and hang it where everyone can see it:

- What method of gaining wisdom is described?
- What is the purpose of gaining that wisdom?
- What are the dangers of not gaining wisdom?

When groups finish reading, have them spend five minutes answering the questions for their passages. Encourage groups to take notes on their discussions.

After five minutes, have volunteers read the biblical passages aloud. Then have groups report their discoveries in the passages. When every group has reported, ask the entire

TEACHER TIP

A group of three can participate in the race by having the number two person start the group's race and determine the winner. If you have a group of five, have the fifth person compete alone in the same manner as number three.

TEACHER TIP

You may want to buy extra cereal so you can make treats to serve during the discussion time following the race.

◁ **THE POINT**

class the following questions:

- **What do these passages teach about who can become wise?**

- **What do they teach about where we can discover wisdom?**

- **What do these passages teach about how we become wise?**

Ask for volunteers to read aloud **Ecclesiastes 5:18-20** and **12:13-14.** Then ask the entire class this question:

- **What do these verses teach about why we should live wisely?**

Say: **To increase in wisdom, we need to feed ourselves a well-balanced diet of biblical proverbs and personal observations. As we do, we'll enjoy life more fully and honor God more effectively.**

Have people answer these questions within their groups:

- **How can you use biblical proverbs to grow in wisdom?**

- **How can you use personal observations to grow in wisdom?**

- **What will you do this week to grow in wisdom?**

Say: ▶ **God gave us our minds, and he expects us to use them. So every day we should honor God with our minds by feeding ourselves on every morsel of wisdom God brings our way.**

■

FOR *Even Deeper* DISCUSSION

Form groups of four to discuss the following questions:

- What do you think Proverbs 1:7 implies about the ability of atheists to discover truth about the physical universe? about humanity? about God? How should we respond to the ideas of people who don't believe in God?

- What's the relationship between the truth of the Bible and other sources of truth? How should we resolve apparent conflicts between the Bible and science? the Bible and our experiences?

■ ■

BIBLE INSIGHT

The Hebrew word for wisdom—*hokmāh*—is best understood as "skill" or "ability," not intellectual acumen. The Old Testament uses this word to describe the ability to manufacture holy garments and pagan idols (Exodus 28:3; Isaiah 40:20) and with reference to the capacity to govern well (Genesis 41:33, 39; 1 Kings 3:9, 12). The same word describes what we might call "common sense," which is knowing how to survive and thrive in the different situations of life.

THE POINT▷

Walking in Wisdom

(30 to 40 minutes)

Ask for a volunteer to read **Proverbs 24:30-34** aloud. Then say: **In these few verses we find the three basic steps of gaining wisdom. First, we observe the world around us. Then we reflect on what we've seen. Finally, we state our conclusion in an easily remembered proverb or saying we can apply to our daily lives.** ▶ **God gave each one of us a mind, and he expects us to use our minds. So let's put the wisdom method into practice by walking around outside for five minutes to see what we can learn.**

Keep people in their groups of four. Give everyone a pencil and an index card. Tell group members to walk around outside for five minutes observing nature and human activity and jotting down what they see.

When time is up, call everyone back to the classroom. Then give group members five minutes to discuss what they learned from their observations and to write on their cards at least two proverbs or sayings that summarize what they learned.

After five minutes, have groups read their proverbs to the rest of the class. After each proverb, invite class members to explain how they might apply the proverb to their daily lives. When all the proverbs have been read and applied, have group members discuss the following questions. Ask:

- **What was your reaction to walking around outside in order to gain wisdom?**

- **To what extent can the world around us teach us truth about ourselves? about God?**

- **What does this exercise teach us about how God has revealed his truth to us?**

Say: **The Old Testament wisdom books teach us that** ▶ **God gave us our minds and expects us to use them. God wants us to learn from the world around us as well as from the wisdom literature of the Bible. In both cases, we must observe and think about what we see, identify the principle taught by our observations, and then apply that principle to our own situations. We did that with our walk outside. Now let's apply the same method to several verses in the book of Ecclesiastes.**

Assign **Ecclesiastes 5:18-20** to half the groups and **12:13-14** to the other half. Give each group a sheet of paper. Instruct groups to carefully read and discuss their passages, to write on their papers one or more general truths taught in the passages, and then to write one specific way each truth could be applied to their daily lives.

◀ **THE POINT**

TEACHER TIP

If you have class members who are unable to go outside, have them and their group members look outside through a window or mentally "walk" around by describing what they saw on the way to class.

BIBLE INSIGHT

God, who is the source of all truth, reveals truth to us in several ways. On the one hand, God speaks directly to us through his Word, the Bible. However, God also communicates truth indirectly or generally through his creation. According to Paul, anyone can learn about God simply by observing nature (Romans 1:18-20). Because God is the author of all that is true, we should constantly and confidently look for truth wherever it may be found.

After five minutes, have groups read their passages and report what they learned from those passages. Then have group members discuss the following questions:

- **What was your reaction to reading the Bible in order to gain wisdom?**

- **How is this like learning from the world around us? How is it different?**

- **How can you learn more effectively from the world around you? from the Bible?**

- **How can you more effectively apply what you already know to your daily life?**

T H E   P O I N T ▷

Say: ▷ **God gave us our minds, and he expects us to use them to discover his truth wherever it may be found. As we carefully observe God's world and regularly read God's Word, we'll grow both in wisdom and in the ability to honor God with our minds and our lives.**

■ ■

For *Even Deeper* Discussion

Form groups of four to discuss the following questions:

- Read Proverbs 26:4-5. To what extent are these proverbs contradictory? complementary? What does this indicate about the truth of biblical proverbs? about how we should apply them to our lives?

- To what extent does God always want us to follow truths revealed in his world? truths revealed in his Word? When might God want us to do something that could be considered unwise? Why might God want us to do this?

■ ■

Apply·It·To·Life™
This Week!

The "Apply-It-To-Life This Week!" handout (p. 48) helps people further explore the issues uncovered in today's class. Give everyone a photocopy of the handout. Encourage class members to take time during the coming week to explore the questions and activities on the handout.

CLOSING

Both Sides of the Story

(up to 10 minutes)

Hang two sheets of newsprint side by side where everyone can see them. Write "Biblical" at the top of one sheet and

"General" at the top of the other. Ask people to call out principles and proverbs they learned during class, including folk sayings from the Opening, biblical truths and proverbs they discovered, and any truths revealed by the Bible Exploration and Application activities. As people call out biblical and general truths, write them on the appropriate newsprints.

When you've written at least five truths on each newsprint, give everyone an index card and a pencil. Tell each person to choose from the sheets of newsprint one biblical truth and one general truth to apply to his or her life during the coming week. Then have everyone write the biblical truth on one side of the card and the general truth on the other.

After three minutes, direct group members to share with each other what they wrote. When everyone in the group has shared, have group members pray for each other, asking God to help them look for wisdom wherever it may be found.

When groups finish praying, hold up an index card and say: **Just as there are two sides to this card, there are two sides to God's wisdom. One side is revealed in God's Word, the other in God's world. Since God gave us our minds, he expects us to use them to discover truth everywhere he has revealed it. So take your card home as a reminder not to be one-sided but to seek both sides of God's truth.**

◀ T H E   P O I N T

 For Extra Time

TRUTH FOR TODAY
(up to 10 minutes)

Choose a current issue on which class members are likely to hold differing views. For example, you might select an issue such as the ordination of women, capital punishment, gay rights, abortion, the permissibility of divorce, or school prayer. Divide the class into two groups. Assign the pro side of the issue to one group and the con side to the other. Give each group a sheet of paper and a pencil. Tell groups to list all the reasons they can think of that support their side of the issue. Encourage groups to list reasons found in the Bible *and* reasons discovered in the world around.

After five minutes, have groups present their reasons. Then ask the entire class the following questions:

- **How completely do the reasons listed support one side over the other?**
- **How well do the biblical reasons correspond to the other reasons?**
- **What does this reveal about the relationship between biblical truth and general truth?**

TEACHER

If groups have more than eight members, form smaller groups of eight or fewer. Then assign the pro side of the issue to half the groups and the con side to the other half.

Apply·It·To·Life™
This Week!

True
Wisdom

God gave us our minds, and he
expects us to use them.
**Proverbs 1:1-7; 24:30-34;
Ecclesiastes 5:18-20; and 12:13-14**

Reflecting on God's Word

Each day this week, read one of the following Scriptures and examine what it teaches about wisdom. Then consider how you can apply the message of each passage to grow in wisdom. List your discoveries in the space under each passage.

Day 1: Job 28:1-28. God alone knows where true wisdom may be discovered.

Day 2: Romans 1:18-20. We can learn about God by observing creation.

Day 3: Proverbs 3:13-20. Those who live by God's wisdom will enjoy life.

Day 4: Proverbs 26:4-5. The wise know what is best in each situation.

Day 5: Ecclesiastes 8:16-17. Even the wise don't know what God is doing.

Day 6: Ecclesiastes 9:7-10. The wise enjoy life as God enables them to do so.

Beyond Reflection

Compile your own wisdom book of personal observations and proverbs. To gather material for your book, carry a small notebook in which you can record insightful sayings you hear or instructive situations you observe. In addition, set aside time several times a week to discover more wisdom in the book of Proverbs. At least once a week, write the sayings, observations, and proverbs in your book of wisdom. Then choose one specific way to apply to your life the wisdom you've compiled.

Coming Next Week: Prophetic Insights
(Isaiah 58:1-11; Jeremiah 7:1-15; and Micah 6:1-8)

Permission to photocopy this handout from Group's Apply-It-To-Life™ Adult Bible Curriculum granted for local church use.
Copyright © Group Publishing, Inc., Box 481, Loveland, CO 80539.

48 ■ LESSON 3

Prophetic Insights

Following God sometimes means challenging the status quo.

THE POINT

OBJECTIVES

Participants will
- discover that God values obedience over religious rituals,
- learn and apply principles for interpreting prophecy, and
- commit to challenging the religious status quo as needed.

BIBLE BASIS

Look up the Scriptures for this lesson. Then read the following background paragraphs to see how the passages relate to people today.

The Old Testament prophecies often appear mysterious and intimidating. In many cases, people are uncomfortable with and uncertain of the meaning of the occasionally bizarre imagery and sometimes strange behavior of the prophets (Ezekiel 1:4-14; Isaiah 20:1-6). However, anyone who understands several basic principles regarding the nature and interpretation of prophecy can read even the most intimidating prophetic texts with insight, accuracy, and confidence.

Simply put, prophecy is the communication of a message from God, through a prophet, to a specific audience. God is the source of the message, so it bears his divine authority. The prophet is merely God's voice, God's representative on earth. In most cases, the people actually hearing the prophet speak were the audience to whom God was speaking. Prophets did, on occasion, address future generations, but usually only as an extension of the original audience. Because the prophets spoke primarily to their own generations, their messages were, contrary to popular opinion, more *proclamation* than *prediction*. As a rule, the prophets told people what they should be doing in the present rather than what was going to happen in the future.

With this brief background, we can interpret any prophecy by following three basic steps. First, we must identify and describe the prophet's audience so we can determine to what

TEACHER TIP

To learn more about the Old Testament prophets, read chapter 10 of *How to Read the Bible for All Its Worth*, by Gordon D. Fee and Douglas Stuart; and chapters 1–5 of *How to Read Prophecy*, by Joel B. Green.

BIBLE INSIGHT

The popular notion that prophets predict the future is misleading if not mistaken. A careful reading of the Old Testament prophets reveals that God is the actor in nearly every reference to a future event. In most cases, God threatens future judgment or promises future blessings such as the coming of the Messiah. Therefore, it is imprecise to say that the prophets "predicted" the future. They simply were the means through which God announced what *he* was going to do.

extent the prophecy applies to us today. Second, we should label the different parts of the prophecy. Most prophetic messages include one or more of the following prophetic speech forms: accusation of sin, announcement of judgment, admonition, and promise of blessing. Finally, to help us apply the prophecy to our own lives, we should state what the prophet hoped to accomplish. Was the prophet's intention to uncover sin, to warn of judgment, to give ethical or religious guidance, or to encourage? As we carefully observe what God said to his people in the past, we'll be better able to hear what God is saying to us today.

ISAIAH 58:1-11

Two prophetic speech forms dominate this passage: accusation (verses 2-5) and admonition (verses 6-11). As always, the prophecy originates with God, who commissions his prophet to confront Israel (house of Jacob) with their sins (verse 1). In short, the people are serious about religion but not about God. They think that keeping their religious duties excuses them from meeting their social obligations. However, God rejects religious activities that are not accompanied by righteous lives. Therefore, the people must stop taking advantage of the weak (verses 6, 9b) and start taking care of the needy (verses 7, 10a). Only then will God honor their fasts and answer their prayers.

JEREMIAH 7:1-15

This passage, like Isaiah 58:1-11, contains strong words of admonition (verses 3-7) and accusation (verses 8-11). In addition, verses 12-15 threaten judgment to motivate the people of Judah and Jerusalem to change their ways. Jeremiah, at God's command (verse 2), stood at the entrance to the Jerusalem temple and announced that there is nothing sacred about a temple inhabited by sinful people. So, unless the people started obeying God's commandments (compare verse 9 with Deuteronomy 5:6, 17-20), God would demolish the Jerusalem temple—as he had the one at Shiloh—and deport the people of Judah—as he had the northern kingdom of Israel (see 2 Kings 17:5-23). The only way they could avert this fate was to replace trust in the temple with obedience to God.

MICAH 6:1-8

Although this prophecy is more complex than those of Isaiah and Jeremiah, the same interpretive principles apply. Micah begins with a rhetorical call for the people of Israel to defend themselves before the mountains—the jurors in a trial between God and his people (verses 1-2). With everyone gathered, God states his accusation. In spite of his gracious treatment of Israel, they have continually disobeyed him (verses 3-5; see also 3:1-3, 9-11; 6:9-12). They even distort and debase the sacrificial system God gave them to pay for their sins (verses 6-7). Therefore, Israel has no defense. Their only hope is to change their ways, to obey Micah's admonition to treat others fairly, to love mercy and kindness, and to walk humbly with their God (verse 8).

In all likelihood, many of your class members picture the Old Testament prophets as strange and frightening individuals. To be honest, some prophets match the image. However, since the prophets spoke on behalf of God, their words deserve to be heard even when they make us uncomfortable. Use this lesson to help people discover why they should read the Old Testament prophets and how they can do so with confidence and skill.

THIS LESSON AT A GLANCE

Section	Minutes	What Participants Will Do	Supplies
OPENING	up to 10	**TO SPEAK OR NOT TO SPEAK**—Discuss times they spoke out against something wrong and times they remained silent.	
BIBLE EXPLORATION AND APPLICATION	25 to 35	☐ Option 1: **GOD'S WORD FOR TODAY**—Write "prophetic" messages for today, study Isaiah 58:1-11 and Jeremiah 7:1-15, then revise their messages to be more like the biblical patterns.	Bibles, pencils, paper, newsprint, marker, tape
	30 to 40	☐ Option 2: **PROPHETIC PRIORITIES**—List their most important spiritual activities, then study Isaiah 58:1-11 and Micah 6:1-8 to learn how to interpret prophecy and to discover what God thinks is important.	Bibles, "Prophetic Priorities" handouts (p. 59), index cards, pencils, offering plate, newsprint, marker, tape
CLOSING	up to 10	**VITAL ACTIVITIES**—Discuss how they can challenge the status quo by changing empty rituals into vital spiritual activities.	Index cards, pencil, offering plate
⏱ **FOR EXTRA TIME**	up to 10	**BOTH SIDES OF THE STORY**—Study prophetic passages of promise and hope.	Bibles, pencils, paper, newsprint, marker, tape
	up to 10	**SIMON SAYS, "PRAY!"**—Play a religious version of Simon Says and compare the game to following the religious status quo in real life.	
	up to 10	**COURSE REFLECTION**—Complete sentences to evaluate the course.	

To Speak or Not to Speak

(up to 10 minutes)

Form pairs. Instruct partners to take turns describing a time they spoke out against something they knew was wrong. For example, one person may have written a letter to the local newspaper, another may have challenged unethical practices at work.

After two minutes, have partners take turns describing a time they saw something wrong and chose not to speak out. Allow two minutes for discussion, then ask for volunteers to share examples of each situation. Then ask the entire class the following questions:

- **What were your emotions when you spoke out? when you kept silent?**

- **What were your main reasons for speaking out? for remaining silent?**

- **What were the positive results of speaking out? of keeping silent?**

- **What were the negative effects of speaking out? of keeping silent?**

T H E   P O I N T ▷ Say: **Probably everyone here recognizes that** ▷ **following God sometimes means challenging the status quo. But it's often difficult to know when to speak out and when to keep quiet. So today we're going to examine the example and teachings of the Old Testament prophets to discover when and how God wants us to challenge the status quo.**

BIBLE EXPLORATION AND APPLICATION

☐ **OPTION 1:**

God's Word for Today

(25 to 35 minutes)

Have each pair join another pair to form a group of four. Give each group a sheet of paper and a pencil. Say: **The biblical prophets are prime examples of people who knew when and how to speak out. They courageously told the people of their day precisely what God wanted them to hear. Let's imagine for a few minutes that we are God's prophets for today. What do you think God's message to people today might be?** Pause. **Discuss with** your group members what you think God wants to say to people today. Then, as a group, write a one-paragraph prophetic message. In five minutes, you'll proclaim your message to the rest of the class.

When time is up, instruct groups to read their messages. Then have group members discuss the following questions. After each question, ask for volunteers to report their groups' responses. Ask:

- **What was it like to assume the role of a prophet?**

- **How would it feel to read your message in public?**

- **In what ways were our messages alike? different?**

- **What does this reveal about our views of prophecy?**

Say: **The Old Testament prophets recognized that ▶following God sometimes means challenging the status quo. But in many cases the status quo they challenged is not the one we would expect. Let's examine two biblical passages to discover what the prophets said and who they said it to.**

Assign **Isaiah 58:1-11** to half the groups and **Jeremiah 7:1-15** to the other half. Have groups read their passages. While groups are reading, write the following questions on a sheet of newsprint and hang it where everyone can see it:

- To whom is the prophet addressing his message?
- Of what sins does the prophet accuse the people?
- What does the prophet instruct the people to do?

When groups finish reading, allow them five minutes to answer the questions for their passages. When time is up, ask for volunteers to read the passages aloud. Then have groups report what they discovered. After groups report, have group members discuss the following questions:

- **How were the biblical prophecies and our prophetic messages alike? different?**

- **How might we modify our views of prophecy in light of the biblical evidence?**

- **What can the biblical prophets teach us about challenging the status quo?**

- **In what specific way might God want you to challenge the status quo?**

Instruct groups to revise their prophetic messages as needed to reflect the biblical perspective. After five minutes, have groups read their new messages.

Say: **▶Following God sometimes means challenging the status quo. But we need to make sure that the status quo we're challenging is the one God wants to be challenged. If we follow the example of the Old Testament prophets, we'll be sure to look inward and**

◀ T H E   P O I N T

BIBLE INSIGHT

Isaiah 58:1-11 presents two views of fasting. The people, on the one hand, believe that going without food on certain religious holidays satisfies God's requirements for fasting (verses 3-5). God, on the other hand, instructs his people to give up their oppressive control over the weak and to share their food, shelter, and clothing with the people who need it. True fasting, according to this passage, is both a religious and a social obligation that involves doing without certain "rights" as an act of devotion to God and service to others.

◀ T H E   P O I N T

address problems in the church before we look outward and attack those in the world.

For *Even Deeper* Discussion

Form groups of four to discuss the following questions:

● What are the modern religious equivalents to fasting (Isaiah 58:1-11)? to the temple (Jeremiah 7:1-15)? How do we sometimes transform these religious institutions into hollow rituals? How can we keep them vital and meaningful?

● Do you think God still speaks through prophets today? Why or why not? How might prophets today be like biblical prophets? How might they be different? How can we tell if someone is actually a prophet from God?

☐ Option 2:
Prophetic Priorities
(30 to 40 minutes)

Before class, make one photocopy of the "Prophetic Priorities" handout (p. 59) for each class member.

Give everyone an index card and a pencil. Have each person write on the card what he or she regards as the two most important spiritual activities. For example, people might list praying, reading the Bible, sharing their faith, or similar activities.

While people are writing, hang a sheet of newsprint where everyone can see it. After two minutes, pass around an offering plate and invite people to "give" their spiritual activities to God by placing their cards in the offering plate. When all the cards have been collected, ask for a volunteer to read what people wrote. Record on the newsprint the activities people named and the number of times each activity was listed.

When all the cards have been recorded, read the list aloud. Then have the pairs from the Opening join together to form groups of four. (If you completed Option 1, keep people in their groups of four.) Have group members discuss the following questions. After each question, ask for volunteers to report their groups' responses. Ask:

● **How did it feel to give your spiritual activities to God?**

● **How do you think God feels when we perform those acts?**

● **What does the list reveal about what we think is important?**

● Why do you think we view these acts as most important?

Say: **It's easy to assume that the spiritual activities we regard as important are also important to God. However, that's not always the case. We don't always see things exactly as God does. So let's examine two Old Testament prophetic texts to learn what God says is important to him.**

Assign **Isaiah 58:1-11** to half the groups and **Micah 6:1-8** to the other half. Give everyone a copy of the "Prophetic Priorities" handout. Instruct group members to follow the instructions at the top of the handout.

After 10 minutes, ask for volunteers to read their Scriptures aloud. Then have groups report what they discovered. When every group has reported, direct group members to discuss the following questions:

● **What do these passages teach is most important to God?**

● **What religious activities are of less importance to God?**

● **How is God's list similar to ours? How is it different?**

● **How can you avoid the sins that the prophets denounce?**

● **What is one way you can obey the prophets' instructions?**

Say: **According to the prophets, ▶following God sometimes means challenging the status quo. In fact, we learn from Isaiah and Micah that we should challenge even our favorite religious activities when they dishonor God and distort his values. By applying the same interpretive principles we used earlier to other prophetic passages, we can discover in greater detail what God regarded as important in the past and what he thinks is important today.**

BIBLE INSIGHT

Prophetic accusations of sin are noteworthy in several ways. First, the prophets rarely condemn sin in principle or in general. In most cases they name specific sins that their audiences are committing. Second, the prophets generally balance their negative accusations with positive instructions. Denunciation of sins can become little more than self-righteous rhetoric when it is not accompanied by moral guidance. Therefore, the prophets usually told the people what they should do *and* what they shouldn't do.

TEACHER TIP

To help people compare their important spiritual activities with what God views as important, hang a sheet of newsprint beside the newsprint you hung earlier in the activity and write the answers to the first question on it.

◀ THE POINT

■ ■

FOR *Even Deeper* DISCUSSION

Form groups of four to discuss the following questions:

● How can we tell when a prophecy is from God? What are the characteristics of true prophecy? What clues might indicate that a prophecy is false? How should we respond when people claim that God told them to tell us something?

● How can we balance challenging a sinful status quo with obeying those with authority over us? When should we challenge the status quo by privately speaking to those in authority? by speaking out publicly?

■ ■

Apply·It·To·Life™
This Week! The "Apply-It-To-Life This Week!" handout (p. 60) helps people further explore the issues uncovered in today's class. Give everyone a photocopy of the handout. Encourage class members to take time during the coming week to explore the questions and activities on the handout.

CLOSING

Vital Activities

(up to 10 minutes)

Before class, write the following words on separate index cards: worship, prayer, fellowship, Bible study, missions, outreach. Make one card for every four people, repeating the words as needed. Place the cards in an offering plate.

Say: **Sometimes the best way to challenge the status quo is to change it into what God wants it to be. So let's close today's lesson by discussing how we can use the gifts God has given us to keep our faith vital and alive.**

Pass around the offering plate, telling each group to take one card. Then have group members discuss the following questions. After each question, ask groups to name their spiritual activities and to report their answers to the rest of the class. Ask:

● **What is one positive contribution of your spiritual activity?**

● **What is one way this activity can become an empty ritual?**

● **What can we do to keep this activity vital and meaningful?**

Then have group members pray for each other, asking God to help them challenge the status quo when they should and to change it into something positive when they can.

T H E   P O I N T ▷

Say: **There's nothing wrong with the status quo when it honors God and helps people. But the prophets show us that ▷following God sometimes means challenging the status quo. During the coming week, ask God to give you the courage and the wisdom to challenge the status quo in a positive and effective way.**

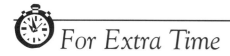

For Extra Time

BOTH SIDES OF THE STORY
(up to 10 minutes)

The Old Testament prophets generally balanced their messages of sin and judgment with words of promise and hope. To help class members better understand and interpret prophecy, have them study one or more of the following texts: Isaiah 43:1-13; Jeremiah 31:27-37; Ezekiel 33:10-20; Hosea 2:1-23; Joel 2:18-32; or Micah 7:8-20.

Form groups of four. Give each group a sheet of paper and a pencil. Assign each group a biblical passage. While groups read their passages, write the following instructions on a sheet of newsprint and hang it where everyone can see it:

- Audience: Identify and describe who the prophet is talking to.
- Message: Label the different parts of the prophet's message.
- Intention: Explain what the prophet wanted the audience to do.

Instruct groups to supply the information for their passages. After five minutes, ask groups to report what they discovered. Then ask the entire class how each passage applies to their lives today. If time permits, have groups read and interpret additional prophetic texts.

SIMON SAYS, "PRAY!"
(up to 10 minutes)

Ask everyone to stand. Then lead people in a game of Simon Says in which some of the instructions are religious activities. For example, in addition to giving instructions such as "Touch your nose," "Shake your leg," and "Rub your stomach," tell everyone, "Say a prayer," "Read your Bible," "Worship God," or "Say something nice to your neighbor."

Play for five minutes or until you have a winner. Then form groups of four to discuss the following questions:

- **How do you feel about the religious acts you performed?**
- **What do you think is God's opinion of those religious acts?**
- **How are these acts like the ones we perform every day? How are they different?**
- **How is following the status quo like playing Simon Says? How is it different?**

TEACHER TIP

If you didn't complete Option 2, read aloud the information in the FYI box on the "Prophetic Priorities" handout (p. 59) before you have people answer the questions.

COURSE REFLECTION
(up to 10 minutes)

Ask class members to reflect on the four lessons on the Old Testament. Then have them take turns completing the following sentences:

- Something I learned in this course was...
- If I could tell friends about this course, I'd say...
- Something I'll do differently because of this course is...

Then ask people what they liked most about the course and how they might change the course. Please note their comments (along with your own) and send them to Adult Curriculum Editor, Group Publishing, Dept. PD, Box 481, Loveland, Colorado 80539. We want your feedback so we can make each course we publish better than the last. Thanks!

Prophetic Priorities

Working as a group, read the information in the FYI box and your assigned biblical passage. Then complete the instructions below for your passage. After 10 minutes, you'll report your conclusions to the rest of the class.

Isaiah 58:1-11

AUDIENCE: Identify and describe who the prophet is speaking to.

MESSAGE: Label the different parts of the prophet's message.

INTENTION: Explain what the prophet wanted the audience to do.

Micah 6:1-8

AUDIENCE: Identify and describe who the prophet is speaking to.

MESSAGE: Label the different parts of the prophet's message.

INTENTION: Explain what the prophet wanted the audience to do.

Apply·It·To·Life™
This Week!

Reflecting on God's Word

Each day this week, read one of the following prophecies and examine what God said to his people in the past. Then consider how you can apply that message to your life today. List your discoveries in the space under each passage.

Day 1: Ezekiel 18:1-32. God promises to treat each person as he or she deserves.

Day 2: Hosea 1:1–2:1. God rejected his people but promised to restore them.

Day 3: Amos 4:1-13. God will punish his people for refusing to return to him.

Day 4: Micah 3:1-12. God turns his back on people who oppress the powerless.

Day 5: Haggai 2:10-19. Holy work doesn't make us good, but we can make it bad.

Day 6: Malachi 1:6–2:9. God rejects offerings when they are less than our best.

Beyond Reflection

Follow the example of the prophets by challenging the status quo around you. Observe how people in your family, your church, your workplace, or society typically act or think. Then think about why people are acting as they do. If you uncover any action or attitude that needs to be changed, commit yourself to challenging that status quo. Before you act, however, ask God to give you the courage and the wisdom to challenge the status quo in a way that would honor him and help others.

Legal Principles

The Old Testament law teaches us how to love God and other people.

Use the active learning principles described in the course "Introduction" (pp. 5-13) and modeled in Lessons 1 through 4 to create your own lesson on Old Testament law. Incorporate the following lesson objectives, Bible Basis information, and activity ideas to help people understand and apply Old Testament law to their own lives.

◀ **THE POINT**

OBJECTIVES

First, people need to recognize that, although they are no longer bound by the Law (Galatians 3:23-25), it is still an important part of their Bibles. Jesus himself commands us to follow the principles behind the individual laws (Matthew 5:17-48), so we cannot ignore Old Testament legal texts.

When people recognize the place of the Law today, they are ready to interpret and apply specific commands to their own lives. To that end, the lesson should teach people the basic principles of interpreting the Law (see the Bible Basis section) and then allow them to use those principles on one or more legal passages. Finally, the lesson should also provide a conceptual framework for understanding and applying specific laws. That is, the lesson should help people discover that the commands show us either how to love God or how to love people (see Matthew 22:34-40; Mark 12:28-34.

BIBLE INSIGHT

The Hebrew noun *tōrāh*, the most common Old Testament word for "Law," derives from the verb *yārāh*, which means "to throw, shoot, direct, or teach" (see Exodus 15:4; 19:13; 35:34; Deuteronomy 17:10, 11; 24:8; Proverbs 4:4, 11). In light of this, we should understand *tōrāh* more as "direction" or "instruction" than "law" in the modern sense. Although the Old Testament law regulated the Israelites' behavior, its primary function was to instruct them. Therefore, Christians, who are no longer under the Law's regulations, can still learn from the truths contained within God's law.

BIBLE BASIS

The interpretation and application of Old Testament commands require at least three steps. First, we must explain the meaning and the purpose of the law for its original audience, the Israelites. In short, we have to determine what God commanded the people to do and why he ordered them to do it. Second, we should identify the theological and ethical principles that the command expressed when it was first given. To do this, we must dig below the cultural details of the command until we reach the foundational truths on which it rests.

When we understand the theology and the purpose of a law,

we are ready to apply it to our lives. In a few cases, application begins with simple obedience to the command as it is written (see Exodus 20:13-16). However, because every law is based upon a more foundational principle, it's never enough simply to do what the Law requires. Rather, in every case we should follow Jesus' example of incorporating the principles and purposes of the Law into every area of our lives (see Matthew 5:21-48). As we do, we will discover that the Old Testament law can teach us how to love God and other people even today.

Exodus 20:1-17

Most people have little trouble meeting the basic requirements of at least most of the Ten Commandments. However, that doesn't mean that they are living by the principles behind these laws. The first four commands were given to promote love for God, the last six to foster love for others, but many people obey all 10 commands with little love either for God or for other people. Instead of adopting the values that the commands embody—values such as respect for life, the family, and truth—people often satisfy themselves with meeting the minimum demands of the Law. In so doing, they fail to obey the Ten Commandments as God intended.

Leviticus 25:8-17, 39-46

The laws regulating the year of jubilee are not as easy to apply as the Ten Commandments. However, the principles underlying these laws are as relevant today as ever. Every 50th year, the people were to return fields to their original owners (verses 10, 13-17) and Israelite slaves to their families (verses 10, 39-46). From this we learn that God's ownership of all things limits our rights over our possessions. We should not accumulate wealth or exercise power when doing so harms others. In addition, God expects us to treat others as graciously as he treats us. At all times we should work for the common good and not simply our own gain.

ACTIVITY IDEAS

Opening: Have people share rules they had to obey as children and as teenagers. Then have people discuss to what extent they obey those rules today and to what extent they abide by the principles behind the rules.

Bible Exploration and Application: Form small groups. Give half the groups sets of instructions to create something useful (a poster praising God or refreshments for the class). Give the other half instructions that accomplish nothing. After people follow the instructions, ask them how they felt about their tasks, how the instructions are like and unlike God's law, and what the purpose of God's law is. Then show people how to interpret the biblical texts so they can discover how God's laws help us love God and other people.

Closing: Ask each person to choose one way to love God and one way to love others during the upcoming week.

Fellowship and Outreach Specials

Use the following activities any time you want. You can use them as part of (or in place of) your regular class activities, or you might consider planning a special event based on one or more of the ideas.

Living Traditions

Many of the Old Testament traditions are still practiced by the Jewish people today. To broaden class members' understanding of the Old Testament, ask a local rabbi or the leader of a Messianic synagogue to discuss and even present some of those practices. For example, you might ask a rabbi to conduct a Passover service or talk about the place of the Law in modern Judaism. The class may even want to visit a local synagogue to observe one of the services. Remind people to treat everyone they meet and everything they see respectfully, seeking only to understand the Jewish traditions more fully than they already do.

Ancient Stories, Modern Truths

Form a Bible study at which people can practice interpreting Old Testament stories *and* learn more about those stories by viewing one of Group's Ancient Secrets of the Bible videos. Each time you meet, have group members apply the interpretive principles to one of the stories listed below. Then watch the corresponding video to gain background and perspective on the story. Conclude by discussing how well the video experts understood the story and how you can apply the truths of the story to your daily lives.

- Genesis 11:1-9, video: *Tower of Babel: Fact or Fiction?*
- Genesis 18:16–19:29, video: *Sodom and Gomorrah: Legend or Real Event?*
- Exodus 14:1-31, video: *Moses' Red Sea Miracle: Did It Happen?*
- Joshua 6:1-27, video: *Walls of Jericho: Did They Tumble Down?*
- Judges 13:1–16:31, video: *Samson: Strongman Hero or Legend?*
- 1 Samuel 17:1-58, video: *Battle of David and Goliath: Truth or Myth?*
- Daniel 3:1-30, video: *The Fiery Furnace: Could Anyone Survive It?*

Challenging Prayers

Combine prayer, fellowship, and the prophetic challenge to the status quo. Once a month, hold a prayer service for some group that is often neglected by the church or rejected by society. For example, pray for AIDS patients, people who have physical or mental disabilities, men and women in prison, people living in care centers, the homeless, or unwed mothers. After the prayer time, serve refreshments and discuss how you can put your prayers into practice by reaching out to and helping the people you prayed for. Encourage class members to continue praying for those people and to minister to them in whatever way they can.

Class Wisdom

Ask people each to record in a journal any insightful sayings they hear, any enlightening situations they observe, or any biblical proverbs that are especially meaningful to them. After one month, have participants meet to share what they've learned. Ask people to explain how applying their insights helps them enjoy life more and serve God better. Then set out supplies such as colored index cards, paper, pens, markers, scissors, tape, and staplers so people can work together to create a booklet of class wisdom. Serve refreshments for people to enjoy while they work.

Changing the Status Quo

To put the teaching of Isaiah 58:6-10 into practice, form task forces to help the groups listed: the oppressed, the hungry, the homeless, those with inadequate clothing, and the afflicted. Instead of offering short-term assistance, commit to helping the people in these groups as long as necessary. Several times a year, assign the groups to new task forces so people can minister to various needs. Meet periodically to report victories and to pray for the needs of the people receiving help as well as the needs of those giving it.

Apply-It-To-Life™ Together

Create a meeting based on the "Apply-It-To-Life This Week!" handouts from the course. As a part of the meeting, ask volunteers to share what they discovered through each of the handouts. During the meeting, have people choose at least two "Beyond Reflection" activities to complete together. Establish a schedule with goals for the completion of each of the activities they select.